As Lovers Always Do

As Lovers Always Do

Marne Wilson

Etchings Press
Indianapolis, Indiana
2019

Copyright © 2019 by Marne Wilson

This publication is made possible by the funding provided by the Shaheen College of Arts and Sciences and the English Department at the University of Indianapolis. Special thanks to those students who judged, edited, designed, and published this chapbook: Kylie Seitz, MacKenzie Estrada, and Maiya Johnson.

UNIVERSITY *of*
INDIANAPOLIS

Published by Etchings Press
1400 E. Hanna Ave.
Indianapolis, IN 46227

All rights reserved

etchings.uindy.edu
www.uindy.edu/cas/english

Printed by IngramSpark

Published in the United States of America

ISBN 978-0-998897-6-6-0

23 22 21 20 19   1 2 3 4 5

Table of Contents

The Tale of the Beds	1
The Moore-Kutcher Jeans Experiment	4
The Recipe File	6
Cyberstalking	7
The Immortal	8
The Greyhound Bus	9
Willpower	12
929 Brookridge	13
Sleigh Ride	14
At Chiaperelli's	15
The Sword in the Stone	17
Hanging Out	18
Communion of the Heart	19
Blame Steve Almond	20
U.S. Highway 85	22
Things I Regret	23
The Gambler	24
The Statue	25
The Fish	26
That Peaceful Easy Feeling	27
The Fruitcake Charm	28
Wanted: One Muse	30
The Beloved	31
To All the Boys Who've Loved Me	32

The Tale of the Beds

During our first year of marriage,
we slept together in a full-size bed.
You complained that I stole all your covers
but tried to pass it off as an affectionate joke.
Every morning, we woke up on opposite sides,
as far apart as humanly possible.
I wondered if this was normal.

During our second year of marriage,
you suggested we upgrade to a queen-size bed.
We no longer needed to escape each other;
the space maintained itself.
There were still good times,
but we no longer felt the need to pretend
that times were good when they were not.

During our third year of marriage,
you decided we would sleep much better
if we each had our own twin-size bed.
We arranged them right next to each other,
like an old-fashioned sitcom couple,
so we could hold hands across the divide.
We promised to visit each other sometimes
but rarely made the effort.

During our fourth year of marriage,
we rearranged the furniture,
pushing our beds against opposite walls.
In my dreams the bedroom became a crypt,
the wall next to me slotted with moldering bodies.
You told me the first winter of our marriage
was the coldest one you ever spent,
and I wondered why you finally mentioned it.
You also told me that I snore.

During our fifth year of marriage,
I started staying up until 3 a.m.,
surrendering myself to that bedroom with you
only when my eyes refused to stay open.
In the mornings you tried to kiss me before leaving for work,
but I turned my face towards the pillow.
In the evenings I watched *The Love Boat*
while you slayed dragons,
our separate fantasies forced to coexist
in one small living room.
We looked for a larger apartment.

During our sixth year of marriage,
I moved to Iowa City.
You couldn't find the time to visit me,
but some weeks I stepped off the Friday afternoon bus,
once more a girl returning from college
bearing dirty laundry and tales of intrigue.
Our bedroom became the cabin of a summer camp
as we stayed up all night giggling and playing cards.
We were the best camp friends ever,
but it always felt good to go home on Sunday afternoon.

During our seventh year of marriage,
you transported my bed,
along with everything else you deemed to be mine,
in a U-Haul truck that you inexpertly parked on my lawn
without bothering to tell me you had arrived.
I had never slept so well in that bed as I did that night,
finally and honestly alone.

The Moore-Kutcher Jeans Experiment

You loved Ashton Kutcher
and imagined you could be just like him.
He'd been discovered in Iowa City
while sitting in the Airliner, your favorite bar.
If you'd been there that night instead,
now it would be you in Hollywood.
You told me this story constantly,
hoping I'd say you were meant to be a star.

Meanwhile, I felt old and washed up,
a failure at two different careers
and also at being a wife.
Iowa City was a chance for me to try on a new life,
and I started with a new pair of jeans.
They made me feel young and adventurous,
no longer a settled married woman,
but a typical college student once more.

So there I was, trying to blend into the computer lab
when you walked in with the latest news of Ashton Kutcher.
"They say he's going out with Demi Moore.
Isn't she, like, way too old for him?"
"Some men have been known to go for older women."
The exchange went over the heads of our preoccupied classmates,
but we both knew a hook had been baited and set.

We need not go into what happened next.
Instead, let's use an old cinematic trick
and skip ahead to the present day.
Ashton and Demi did get married,
but they couldn't make it last,
and now he's married to someone younger than he is.
I was tired of feeling like a cougar,
so I married someone ten years older than I am.
And you? After all the fuss and drama,
you married someone exactly my age in the end.

The Recipe File

When you asked for a few of my recipes,
it seemed like the most intimate request
a man could have made of me,
more personal than if you had asked
to see me without my glasses
or even without my dress.

I never divulge my secrets in the kitchen,
aware that they are my stock in trade
and the only thing that ever gets me invited to parties.

But it was different with you,
who I thought would eventually partake
of three meals a day from my kitchen,
so I gave them to you gladly,
opening my heart along with my cookbook.

Now when I imagine the two of you laughing
in a sleek kitchen straight out of *Better Homes and Gardens*
as you prepare my oven-fried chicken,
my fajita quesadillas,
or my baked Italian pasta dish,
I can only think that I have given you a wedding present
that will stick with both of us for our whole lives.

Cyberstalking

On whitepages.com, I found a list
of every place you've ever lived.
With Google Street View, I saw
what each of those houses looked like.
Wikipedia gave me the median income
of your neighborhood,
while Yelp gave me a ranking
of all your favorite restaurants.
From Facebook I know your top
114 bands and 27 TV shows.

Yet none of these sources can tell me
what it was like
to live in those houses,
to frequent those restaurants,
to hear those bands
or to watch those TV programs.
Nothing can ever tell me
what I need to know—
how you rearranged your life
after I stopped paying attention.

The Immortal

I once proclaimed you to be a mortal and me an immortal,
for I would continue existing in this place forever
while you would quickly move on to the next realm.
I don't become involved with mortals, I said,
for they pass away too quickly,
leaving only anguish in their wake.
Better to look down upon you loftily
from the slopes of Olympus,
taking amusement from your actions
but always remaining detached.

In spite of that noble pronouncement,
I did attach myself to you in the end,
allowing myself to become accustomed to your face
and to measure the worth of my endeavors by its expressions.
Now you are leaving,
and I see that I was wrong from the beginning.
I am the mortal, tied to this one small existence,
while you are the immortal
with the whole world at your feet.

The Greyhound Bus

Two states away they were burying my uncle,
but when I got on a Greyhound bus,
it was heading toward Chicago instead.
I had a job interview there the next day,
one that could have been easily rescheduled,
but as usual I preferred to go off alone
rather than endure the barrage
of my family's blunt questions,
each innocent on its own,
but together as cold and stinging as a sleet storm.

The bus was crowded that day, so I ended up
far in the back with the long-distance travelers.
A man covered in Doritos crumbs
with a teetering stack of Dungeons and Dragons novels
opined on a speech he'd heard the night before
by a young state senator from Illinois.
"44th president of the United States," he predicted cockily,
while everyone nearby snickered and shook their heads.

My eyes met those of a young man across the aisle,
unkempt and smelling of too many things to identify.
Although it was the middle of summer,
he wore a gray wool turtleneck sweater,
just like one my first husband had owned.
After a few minutes of small talk,
he said he was going to Kennebunkport
to visit the Kennedys.
I didn't laugh and didn't even tell him
he had the wrong city.
I think he loved me for that more than anything.

Why did I love him?
After all these years, I still cannot say,
only that something inside me
clung to something inside him,
as unmistakable as it was preposterous.

We spoke desperately of many things that day,
words tumbling out as fast as we could form them.
When the bus stopped, we rearranged things
so we could sit together,
talking harder and faster all the while.
I have no memory of the topics we covered,
only that it felt like a sexual act,
thrusting towards something together
until we finally reached a climax.
Then we fell apart, exhausted, as lovers always do.

While he snored beside me,
I chatted with the man seated behind us.
He told me he liked books about drow elves.
Then he said he was on his way to his uncle's funeral.

Right as we pulled into Chicago,
my busboard lover finally awoke.
He apologized for wasting our time together,
but said it felt much easier to sleep
while I was there to protect him.
In the perpetual chaos of the bus terminal,
he showed me his ticket to Kennebunkport,
then said he wanted to spend the night with me instead.
I knew it would change nothing,
or maybe I was afraid it would change everything.
I said I needed time to think.
    We went outside and sat on the steps of the building

as people shoved their way past us
and tripped over our luggage.
He lit a cigarette and silently smoked
while I thought about a woman I knew.
She married a man she met on a plane
and ruined her life forever.
I told him he should get back on the bus.
We hugged each other long enough
to last for the rest of our lives.
Then I picked up my overnight bag
and walked off down Harrison Street
to the aquarium as I'd planned all along.
I thought of his drab clothes
as I watched the brilliant fish swim by.
I told myself I was glad to be alone once more.

Willpower

Always known for the strength of my will,
I was able to taste desire and defer it in the same breath.
Once I nursed a craving for a chocolate milkshake,
putting it off day after day for three solid years,
then finally letting the idea slip away without ever indulging.

So when we met, it seemed such a small thing,
unimportant really, to deny my desire for you
and pretend that all was well between us.
You wanted to break my ascetic ideals
but only got as far as the ice cream,
convincing me to buy a box of peach melba,
the first I had ever bought just for myself.

Now I eat ice cream daily,
have transmuted unfulfilled desire
into something methodical and controlled,
each precisely measured portion
enough to keep the larger temptation at bay.

But I could never learn this secret with you.
My willpower has kept us apart for ten years now,
and it has become far too late to dream
of scooping you into my cup.

929 Brookridge

I came across it just at twilight,
the perfect house where you and I
could live a perfect life together.
I wanted to rush home
and write the story of that life,
make it true by acting as if
it had already come to pass,
but in truth I could not even imagine
where to begin
or how it could ever become real.
Instead I let the idea remain
vague and hazy in my subconscious,
and after all this time
I can barely remember it,
only the thought of a lamp in the window
and an easy chair and a cat.

Sleigh Ride

Of all the songs in the world,
you picked this one to be ours.
It must have been right before Christmas.
I noticed you humming this tune
whenever you were happy with me,
which was often in those days,
and I asked you what it meant to you.
You said you had no idea,
and I pretended to believe it.

I focused on the romance of the lyrics, but
I should have taken it as a sign
that our bond was for special occasions only,
too fragile to last year-round.
Then again, you did keep singing it
all through that whole first year,
from one Christmas to the next.
"Just hear those sleigh bells jingling,
ring-ting-tingling too…"
But that's as far as you ever got.
Even in song, you could not finish the thought,
bring the line to its logical conclusion.
I did notice that, eventually.

In time, you said the song was torturing you,
asked me to help remove it from your head.
Now you say that you hate winter,
and that you never think of this song at all.

At Chiaperelli's

Even librarians can be spontaneous at times,
so you and I set out without a destination,
sure that any convention city we met in
would have a five-star restaurant
around every corner.

Actually, I suspect you were lying
when you said you had no plan,
for when we reached a certain point,
your pace slowed,
you pretended to be surprised
by the name on the sign above us,
and you said oh-so-casually,
"I've heard this place is good."

However, your secret plans
did not include the other sign,
the one on the door that said
"Closed for private party,"
and so you were forced
to be truly spontaneous.

After a moment's hesitation,
you knocked on the door
and asked the suspicious-eyed waitress
where she would most like to dine
if not in her own establishment.
She gestured vaguely across the street,
and thus we found Chiaperelli's.

The food was good,
but what was better was the conversation,
centered on plans we had for our careers,
but always hinting at other plans
we might eventually share.

Now I wonder if all that talk was
spontaneous or calculated,
a real connection or a pointless sham.

Did you have an agenda for me
that never came to pass,
or were you leading me on
a pleasant walk to nowhere?

The Sword in the Stone

For years I have been wedged into this rock,
waiting for someone to come and liberate me.
As time went on, many tried,
struggling and grunting and becoming red in the face
before finally turning away,
mumbling as they left that they never wanted me anyway.
Many of them have cursed me,
thinking that it was I who would not yield,
would not allow myself to become theirs.
But from my point of view, it was they who had failed.
If only one had been strong enough,
he could have released me from this bondage.
No one knew how much I yearned for each one to succeed,
how much I tried to help each one draw me out.

Now here comes another, young, unassuming,
no different outwardly than the rest,
yet he does not know the fear that he will fail.
His eyes are clear and free of worry; his heart is, too.
He puts his hand on my hilt,
and I feel the power surge through me.
This has never happened before.

I am sure now that he will be the one to win me,
that we will travel together
through countless battles and adventures,
that history will remember both our names.
For I know now who I am.
I am Excalibur, and I have finally met my match.

Hanging Out

Sitting on beanbag chairs in your parents' basement,
we listen to the "Shaggy Dog Cha-Cha-Cha"
on my record of *Disney Dance Tunes*.
Your smiling but unobtrusive mother brings us
tall glass bottles of Coke with straws peeking out,
a pan of brownies,
and, if it's close to suppertime,
a plate of toasted cheese sandwiches.
This is the happiest day of my life,
just hanging out with you.

Too bad this isn't a real memory.
Instead, it comes from a variety of sources:
Nancy Drew books,
Betty Crocker's Guide to Easy Home Entertaining,
nights I spied on my big sister
and afternoons spent with Barbie and Ken.
Bits and pieces of these implanted memories
have formed an image much more perfect
than any actual hanging out either of us have ever done.
I could not expect you to live up to this teenage ideal,
forty years out of date
and twenty-five years too young for us,
but it travels through my mind
every time you say the phrase.

Communion of the Heart

You say that if I give you my heart,
you will keep it safe forever,
locked away in a lacquered box.
Taking it out only on special occasions,
you will never let it be consumed.
This is not what I want at all!

If I give you my heart,
I fully expect that you will give me yours.
Then we will stand facing each other
and bite into them at the same time,
letting the red juice
(as if from a cherry popsicle
or a slice of watermelon)
drip down our chins.
Once finished with this memorial meal,
each of us will have the energy
to grow a new heart in our chest,
a hybrid or chimera of what is best
of both of us.

Blame Steve Almond

that we missed our one shot at sex.

In the library on my lunch break,
I took a shortcut through the stacks,
and a book of his essays fell at my feet.
I couldn't pass up such an obvious sign
and read it religiously each day
until my trip to see you.

The only essay I remember:
what happened when his long-time,
long-distance, long-suffering girlfriend
became pregnant.

He wrote about his constant worry
and feelings of impotence,
but I saw it from the woman's point of view instead:
how I would be left holding the bag,
going to doctor's appointments
and vomiting into wastebaskets
while you rode camels 8,000 miles away.

I didn't want our future offspring
to be born into such resentment,
so I removed all chance of its conception.

Of course, he or she lives on
in the parallel universe of my imagination,
all the more real because of my willful act of negation.
What would have happened if I'd found
an erotic novel that day instead,
spent my lunch hours planning steamy seduction
instead of worrying
about backup birth control and time zones?
What if the door had opened instead of closed?

U.S. Highway 85

You took me driving there once,
eagerly pointing out prairie dog towns
and one-room schoolhouses.
Your mother had already told me
this was your favorite stretch of road out of many,
and I believed it as your face brightened
at sights you must have seen countless times before.

When you flicked an apple core casually
out the open window onto the pavement,
you seemed not litterbug but man on his own property
with dominion over all he surveyed.

Perhaps I appeared disinterested or detached,
but in truth I was so starstruck
to be sitting in your passenger seat
that I could concentrate on nothing else,
letting the scenery wash over me
and focusing on the sound of your voice
and the light in your eyes.

An even earlier memory comes to mind—
me in 7th grade, the only year in all of school
when I didn't even pretend to have a boyfriend.
There I am in Miss Tillema's study hall,
scribbling in my magenta notebook
that I know there is a boy out there made just for me.

But since I have no image of him to focus on,
instead my thoughts are full of scenes
from U.S. Highway 85.

Things I Regret

A brace of Cornish hens that was never eaten.
A burgundy necktie that was never worn.
A Skype microphone that was never connected.

A letter that never arrived.
Another letter that was never sent.

A love poem that was never read.
A fruitcake that was never baked.
A lobster that was never ordered.

A kiss by the raspberry bushes that never happened.
A door in the moonlight that never opened.
A pair of pink pajamas that were seen, but not by you.

Two chairs that were placed too far apart.

Three words that were never said.
Two more that were.

The Gambler

Every attempt at communication
is like dropping a coin into a slot machine.
You hear the clunk as it falls in,
you pull the handle,
and then there is nothing to do but wait.

When you don't get through,
instead of wanting to cut your losses,
your desire to continue only increases.
You know the odds have to turn in your favor.

You begin to rely on secret rituals,
poring through the data for hidden patterns.
"Maybe if I wear pink today."
"Maybe if I don't say anything important at all."
"Maybe if I act like I don't care."
But that last one never works.
Who can act nonchalant
in the noise and glare of a casino?

The humdrum routines of life fall away
and are replaced by new ones:
an exhilarating blur of odds calculations,
crossed fingers,
and sighs too deep for words.

The Statue

When first we met, you were a revelation,
the closest thing to perfection I had yet seen,
as beautiful and flawless as a Grecian statue,
but also as smooth, as seamless, as impenetrable.
There was no point in lingering at your base;
I knew I could find no foothold.

Time has a way of working on marble.
Water and weather erode it, and it loses its first luster.
But yet it is the imperfections in a piece that make it human,
that give it something with which we can identify,
that turn it into something to take home.
And so it was with you.
On closer inspection,
the tiny cracks in your façade became the openings
that I could grab onto and begin to climb.
It was your flaws that gave me room to work,
and your humanity that gave me reason to hope.

But now I view you across a vast distance,
through the lens of a telescope that flattens as it magnifies.
I see only your perfect glimmering whiteness;
I cannot identify anything I could claim as my own.

The Fish

You love fish, and sometimes I think you are one,
darting through any body of water
at the speed of the light that reflects off your scales.
Held up by buoyant force, you pay little attention to gravity,
like an astronaut who has achieved escape velocity
from the earth and all the petty things
that try to hold him here.

Indeed, you are much too smart to fall for the flashy lures
that some use to try to reel you in.
You will become a thing of legend in the tales of fisherwomen
as they sit around the hearth surrounded by grandchildren.

You will have no grandchildren;
fish do not have families, only schools.

That Peaceful Easy Feeling

It only hurts a little bit
when I hear the opening chords on the radio,
Glenn Frey strumming and singing
in such a stereotypical country-western way
that it's a wonder I recognize it so quickly.
My first thought is "I used to like this song,"
but just then he gets to the line that I hate
about sleeping with his woman in the desert,
and my mind flashes to the Facebook picture
that you later deleted,
but could never erase from my mind,
of the luxurious tent in the wadi where you once slept
but not alone.
By then Glenn is singing, "I found out a long time ago,"
and I think that it was five years ago when I found out,
and I should really be over it by now, shouldn't I?
Now he's gotten to the peaceful easy feeling of the title,
and I can still remember the mood this song once evoked in me,
back when it reminded me of a different, venison-eating boy.
I can't believe I've let you ruin this song for me,
and I don't suppose you'll ever realize that,
unless you are reading this poem right now.

The Fruitcake Charm

As a girl, I sought after love magic,
testing every incantation and old wives' tale
that promised to foretell future bliss.
I tossed orange peels over my shoulder,
counted every button on my blouse,
and rotated each apple stem until it broke off.
Once, I even ate a cake of ashes
to see my future husband's face in a dream.

Despite my best efforts,
none of these spells worked,
so when I declared
that any man who tasted my fruitcake
would love me forever,
it seemed like another silly game.
The only boy who ever tried it was
a gormless neighbor.
If he loved me, he never said,
so it did me no good.

But when I found you
and longed to keep you for all time,
although I felt too old for such hokum,
I bought myself some brand new fruitcake pans.
I couldn't find my old and faithful recipe,
so I chose one at random from the cookbook.
It was a complete and total disaster.

The next December I found my old recipe,
right where it should have been all along,
and I made it for a new man
who has been mine ever since.

So now the question I ask myself is this:
did I lose you because of a bad fruitcake,
or did the fruitcake refuse to bless our union?

Wanted: One Muse

I had a very good one once,
one whose every word would click and clack
against others already floating in my brain,
then catalyze them to come together in a granular form,
like iron filings in a petri dish,
until they were easily drawn out
by the magnet of my consciousness.

Yes, he was the best of muses,
but he wanted to be more than that,
and so I set him free to seek a muse of his own.

I have tried to train another,
but the first one, quite promising, eluded my grasp,
and this new one is a noble gas,
as bracing as a lungful of helium
but no use at all as a catalyst for anything
but domesticity and love.

He says I need no muse except myself,
but I find it impossible to rise to the occasion,
and thus I place this ad where anyone may find it.

The Beloved

My eyes scan the horizon for the beloved.
I have done this a thousand times in my life,
for dozens of different boys and men.
What is new is this:
today I think of this one as "the beloved,"
the person who fills that role for the moment.
Why bother to use his name?

Let me ask this question another way.
How many actors have played the Phantom on Broadway,
and does it matter whose face is behind the mask?
The role will be the same no matter who plays it,
and the show will go on for perpetuity.
Likewise, I must take comfort from the fact
that there will always be a beloved,
no matter how many times the role is recast.

To All the Boys Who've Loved Me

I like to think of you gathering in some church basement,
circling the folding chairs in the center of the room
and selecting donut holes and Styrofoam cups of coffee
from the refreshment table in the corner.
Once you're all settled, some brave soul begins.
"Hello, my name is William, and I love Marne."
"Hello, William," everyone responds in unison.
Then he says things I can only guess at,
speaks of long sleepless nights spent pining for my touch
and days when the urge to pick up the phone
almost gets the better of him.

I like to imagine all of you together,
because otherwise it's just too much to bear,
to think of so many men
afflicted with silent burdens of love
while I sit here at my kitchen table,
alone except for my paper and my pen.

Acknowledgements

Grateful acknowledgement is made to the following publications in which these poems first appeared:

Alexandria Quarterly: "Communion of the Heart"

Avatar Review: "The Immortal"

Boston Literary Magazine: "929 Brookridge"

Coachella Review: "U.S. Highway 85"

Constellations: "The Moore-Kutcher Jeans Experiment"

Dime Show Review: "The Greyhound Bus"

Emrys Journal: "To All the Boys Who've Loved Me"

Gargoyle: "Blame Steve Almond"

Mojave Heart Review: "The Sword in the Stone"

Oyez Review: "The Tale of the Beds"

Picaroon Poetry: "Hanging Out"

Sweet Tree Review: "The Recipe File"

Uppagus: "That Peaceful Easy Feeling"

Colophon

All titles are set in Sanvito Pro.
All text is set in Marion.

Author Biography

Marne Wilson's poems have appeared in many journals, including *Poetry East, Atlanta Review, Flint Hills Review, Cold Mountain Review,* and *Hobart*. Her previous chapbook, *The Bovine Daycare Center*, was published by Finishing Line Press in 2015. Originally from rural North Dakota, she previously worked as a reference librarian at Ohio University in Athens and now lives in Parkersburg, West Virginia, with her husband Shane.

Etchings Press

Etchings Press is a student-run publisher at the University of Indianapolis. Each year, student editors choose the Whirling Prize, a post-publication award, in the fall and coordinate a publication contest for one poetry chapbook, one prose chapbook, and one novella in the spring. For more information, please visit etchings.uindy.edu.

Previous winners and publications

Poetry
2019: *As Lovers Always Do* by Marne Wilson
2018: *In the Herald of Improbable Misfortunes* by Robert Campbell
2017: *Uncle Harold's Maxwell House Haggadah* by Danny Caine
2016: *Some Animals* by Kelli Allen
2015: *Velocity of Slugs* by Joey Connelly
2014: *Action at a Distance* by Christopher Petruccelli

Prose
2019: *Dissenting Opinion from the Committee for the Beatitudes* by Marc J. Sheehan (fiction)
2018: *The Forsaken* by Chad V. Broughman (fiction)
2017: *Unravelings* by Sarah Cheshire (memoir)
2016: *Pathetic* by Shannon McLeod (essays)
2015: *Ologies* by Chelsea Biondolillo (essays)
2014: *Static: Stories* by Frederick Pelzer (fiction)

Novella
2019: *Savonne, Not Vonny* by Robin Lee Lovelace
2018: *Edge of the Known Bus Line* by James R. Gapinski
2017: *The Denialist's Almanac of American Plague and Pestilence* by Christopher Mohar
2016: *Followers* by Adam Fleming Petty

www.ingramcontent.com/pod-product-compliance
Lightning Source LLC
Chambersburg PA
CBHW070442010526
44118CB00014B/2153